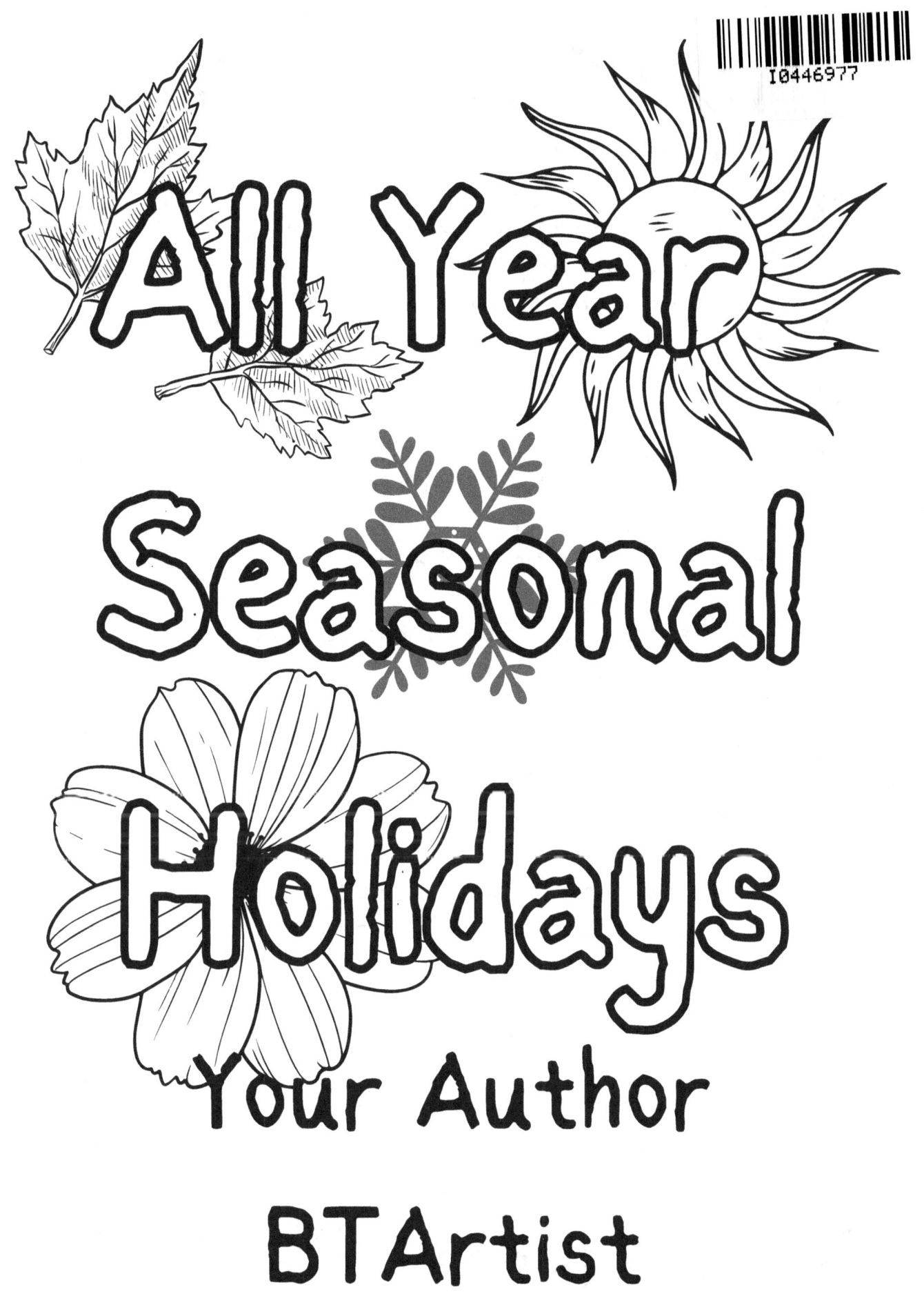

All Year Seasonal Holidays

Your Author

BTArtist

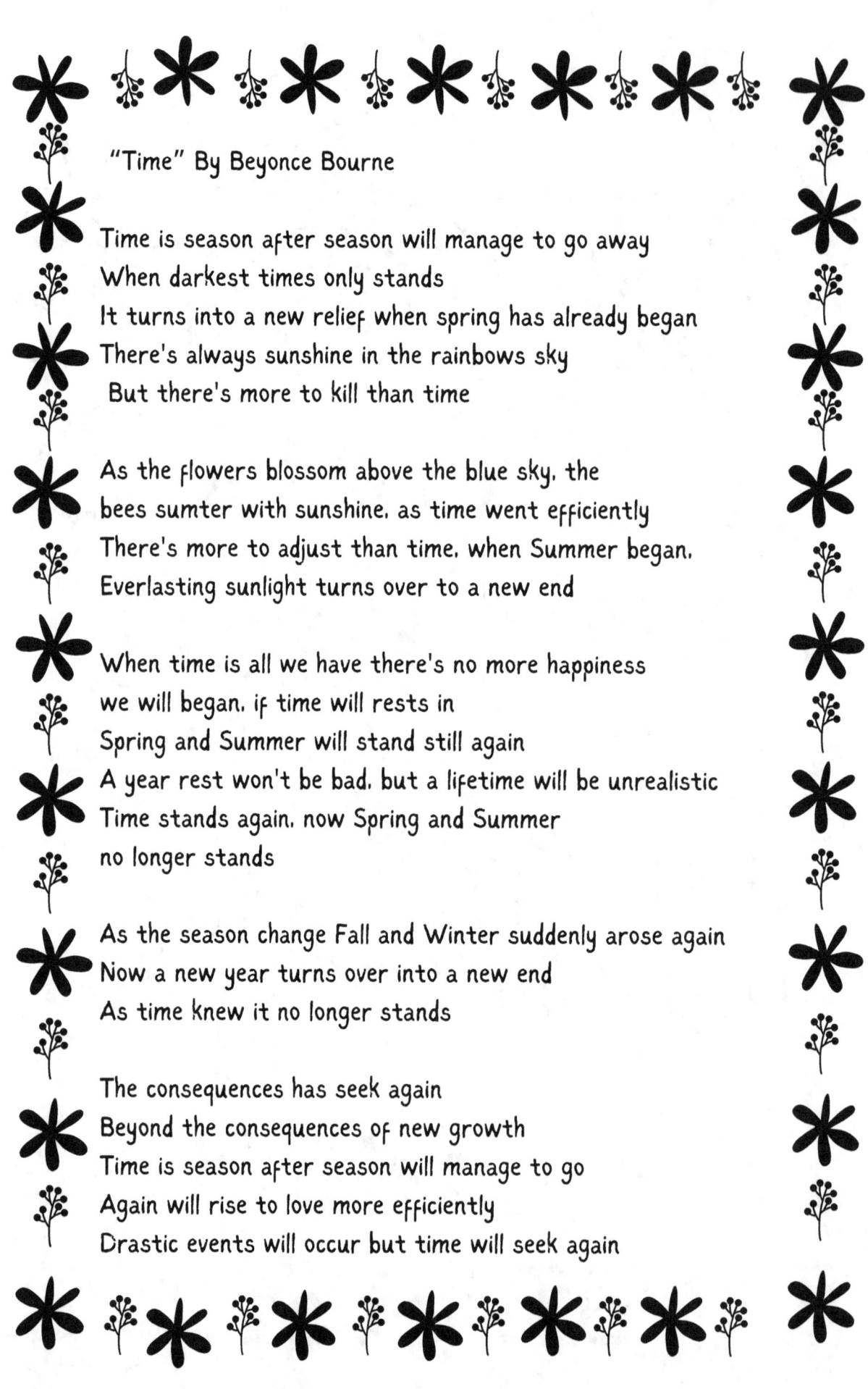

"Time" By Beyonce Bourne

Time is season after season will manage to go away
When darkest times only stands
It turns into a new relief when spring has already began
There's always sunshine in the rainbows sky
 But there's more to kill than time

As the flowers blossom above the blue sky, the
bees sumter with sunshine, as time went efficiently
There's more to adjust than time, when Summer began,
Everlasting sunlight turns over to a new end

When time is all we have there's no more happiness
we will began, if time will rests in
Spring and Summer will stand still again
A year rest won't be bad, but a lifetime will be unrealistic
Time stands again, now Spring and Summer
no longer stands

As the season change Fall and Winter suddenly arose again
Now a new year turns over into a new end
As time knew it no longer stands

The consequences has seek again
Beyond the consequences of new growth
Time is season after season will manage to go
Again will rise to love more efficiently
Drastic events will occur but time will seek again

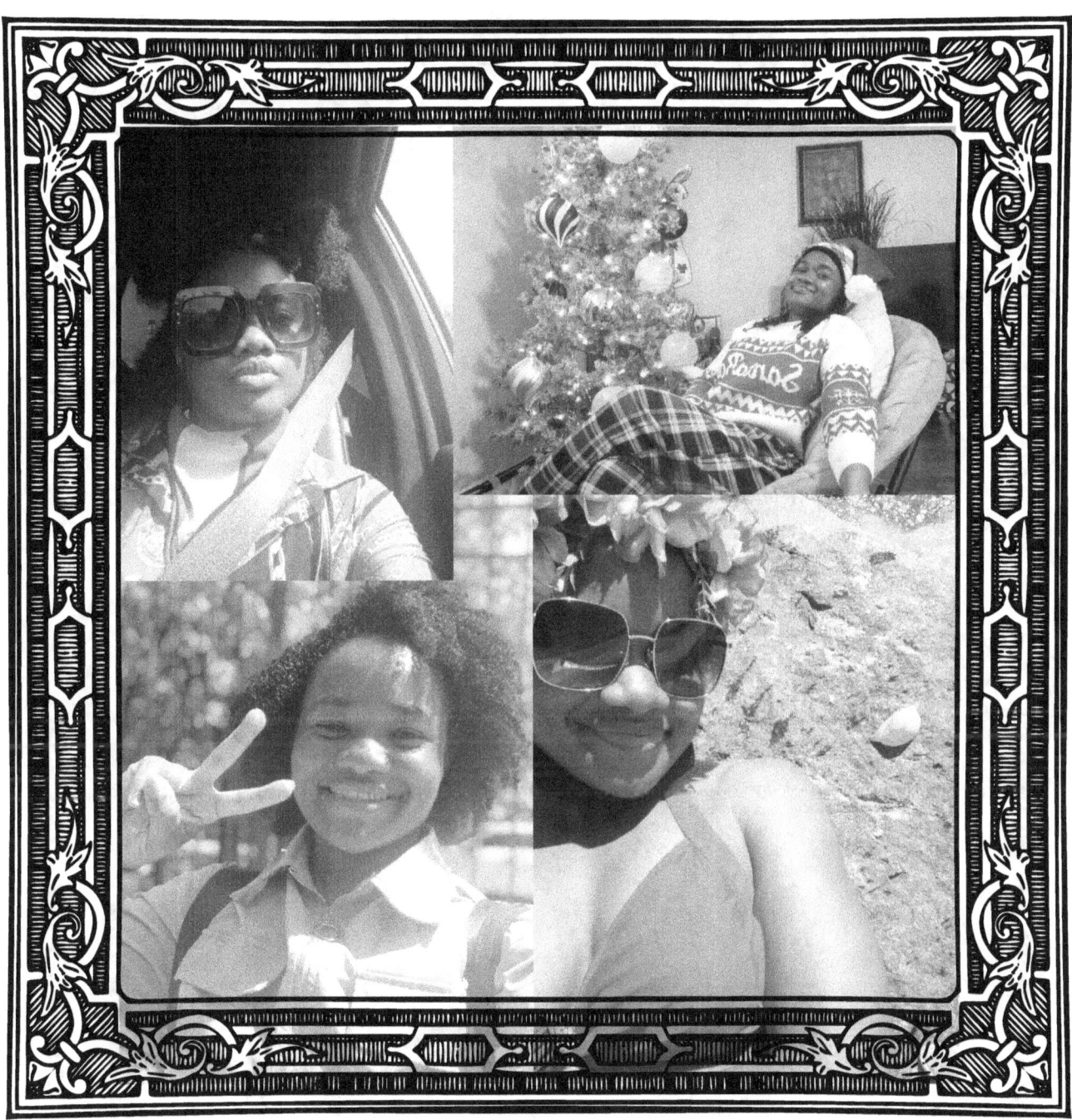

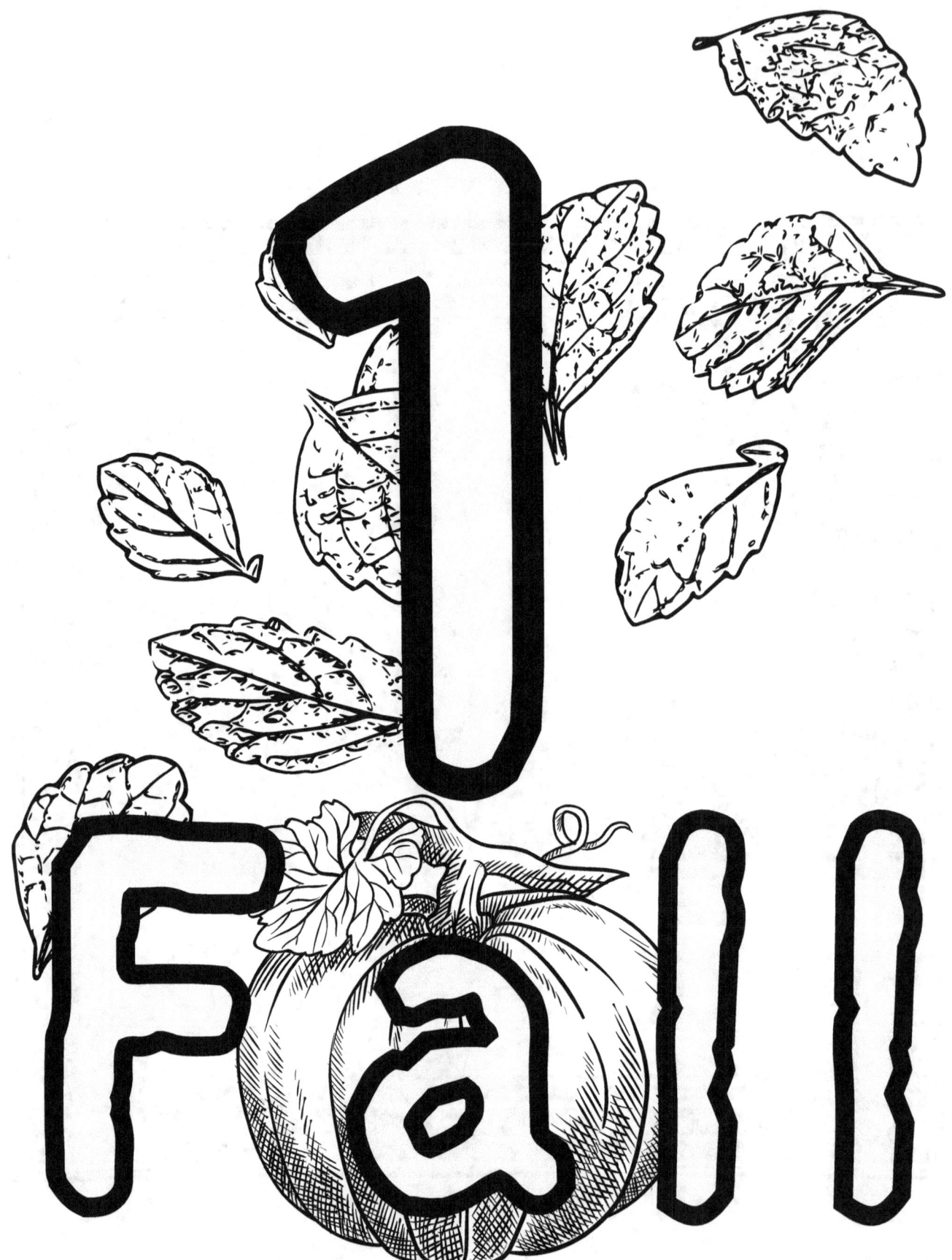

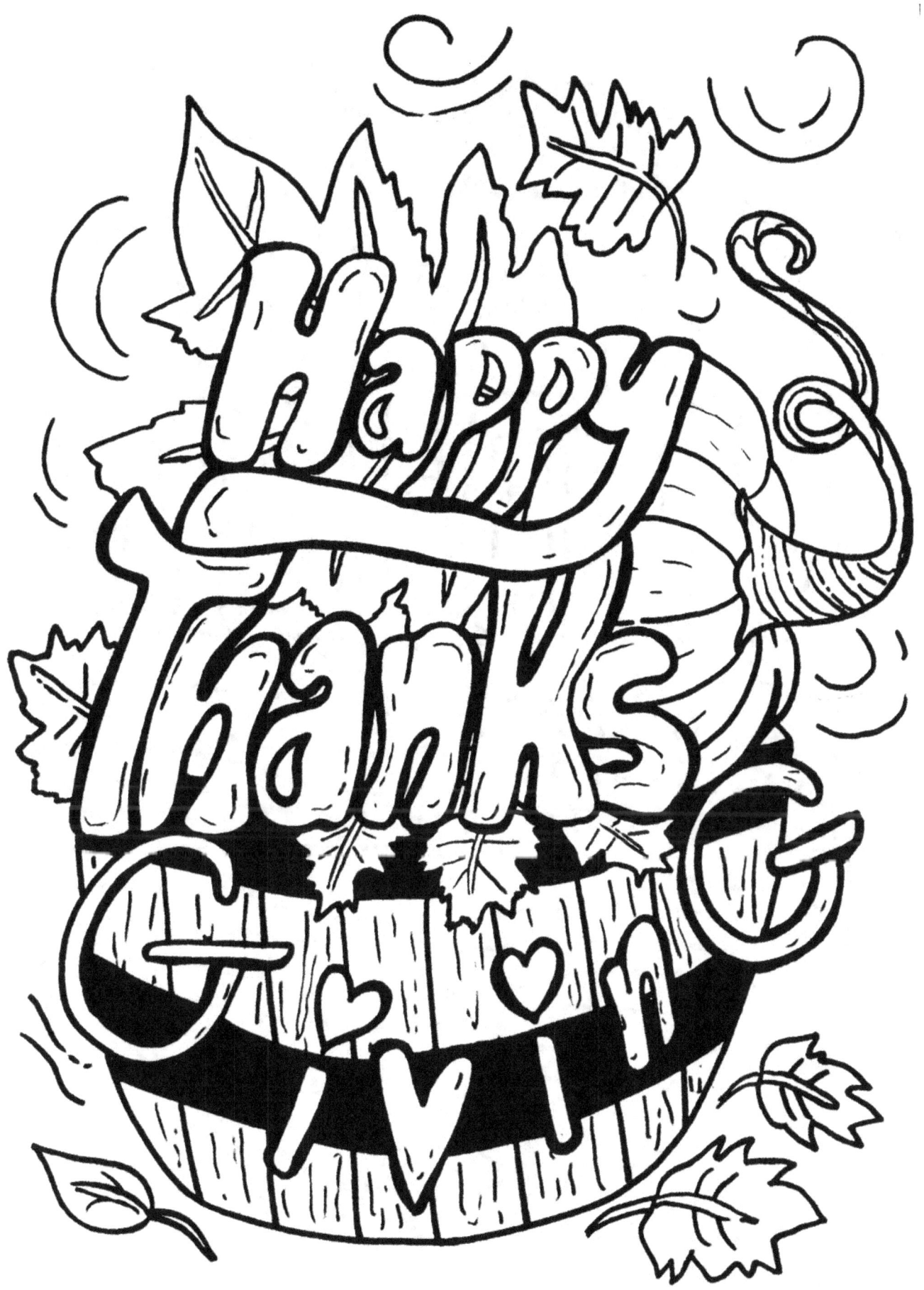

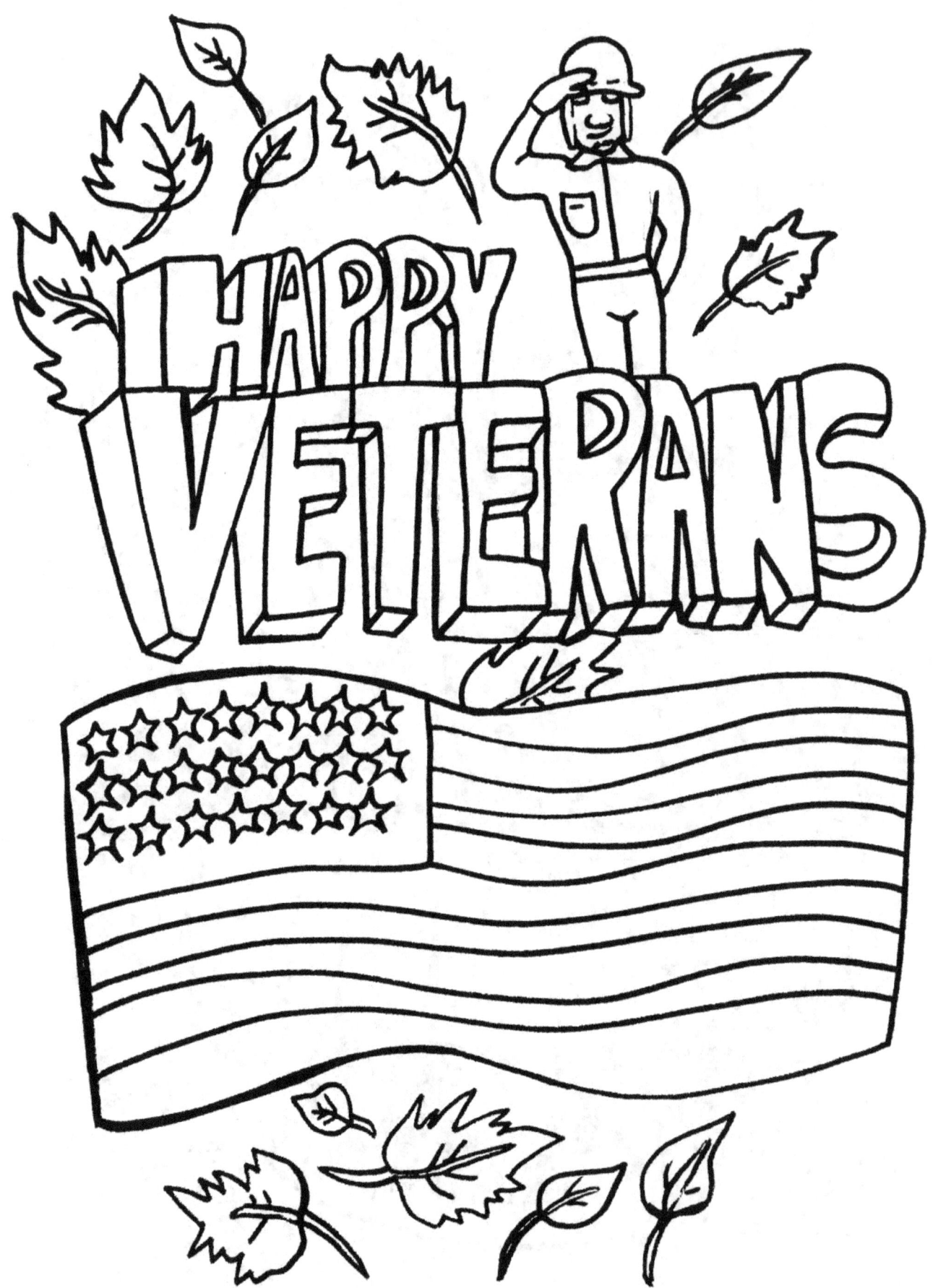

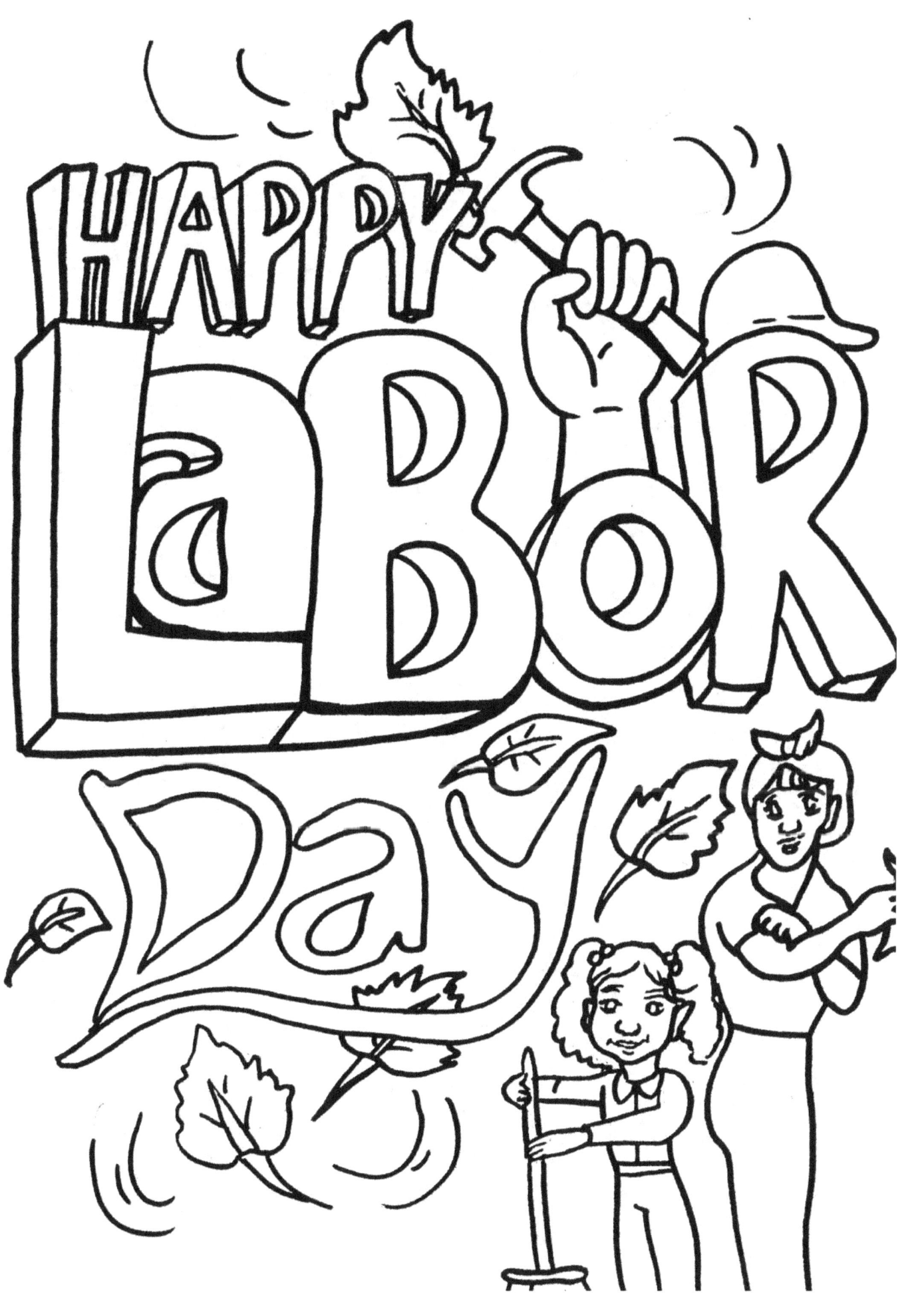

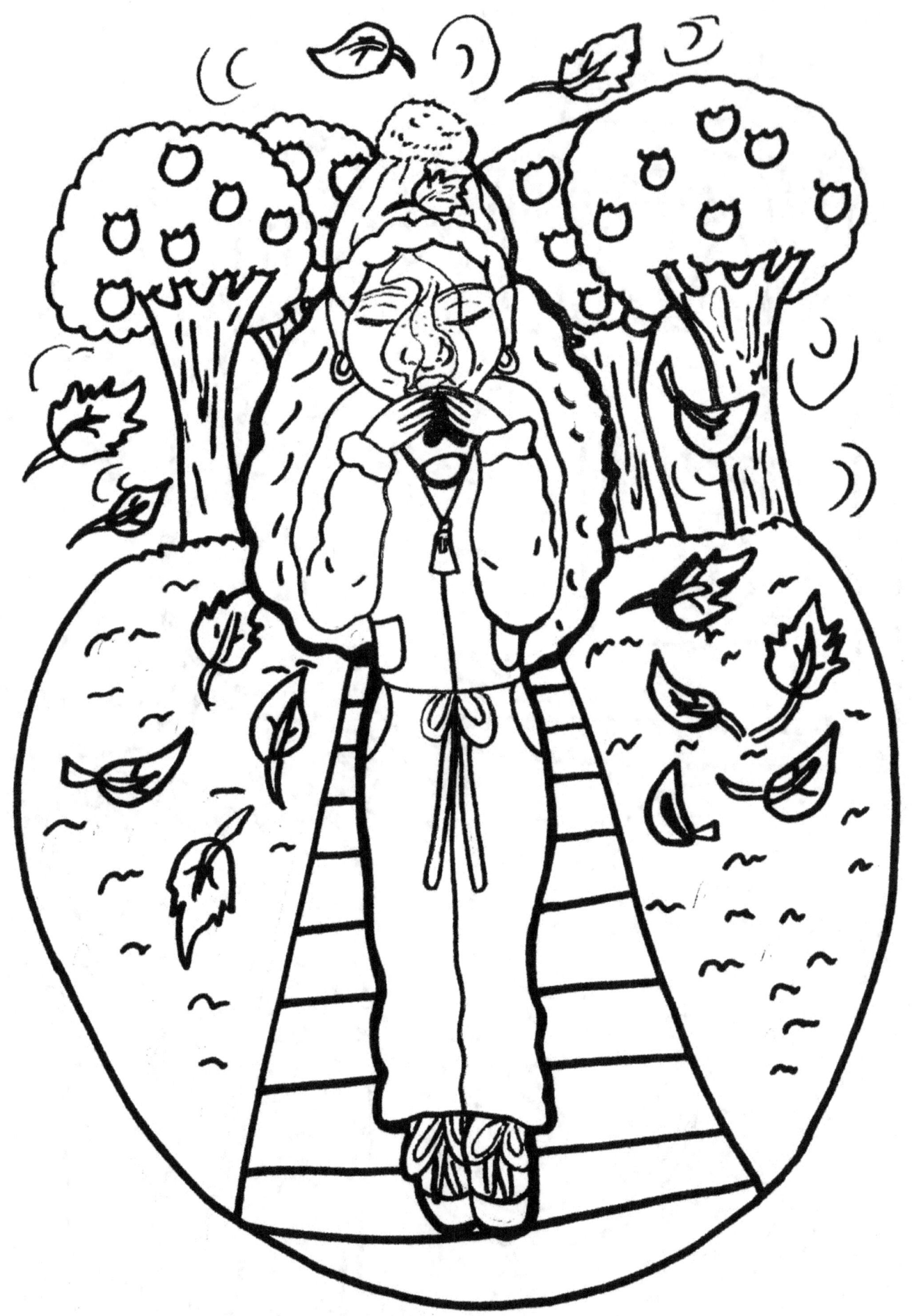

Fall Memories

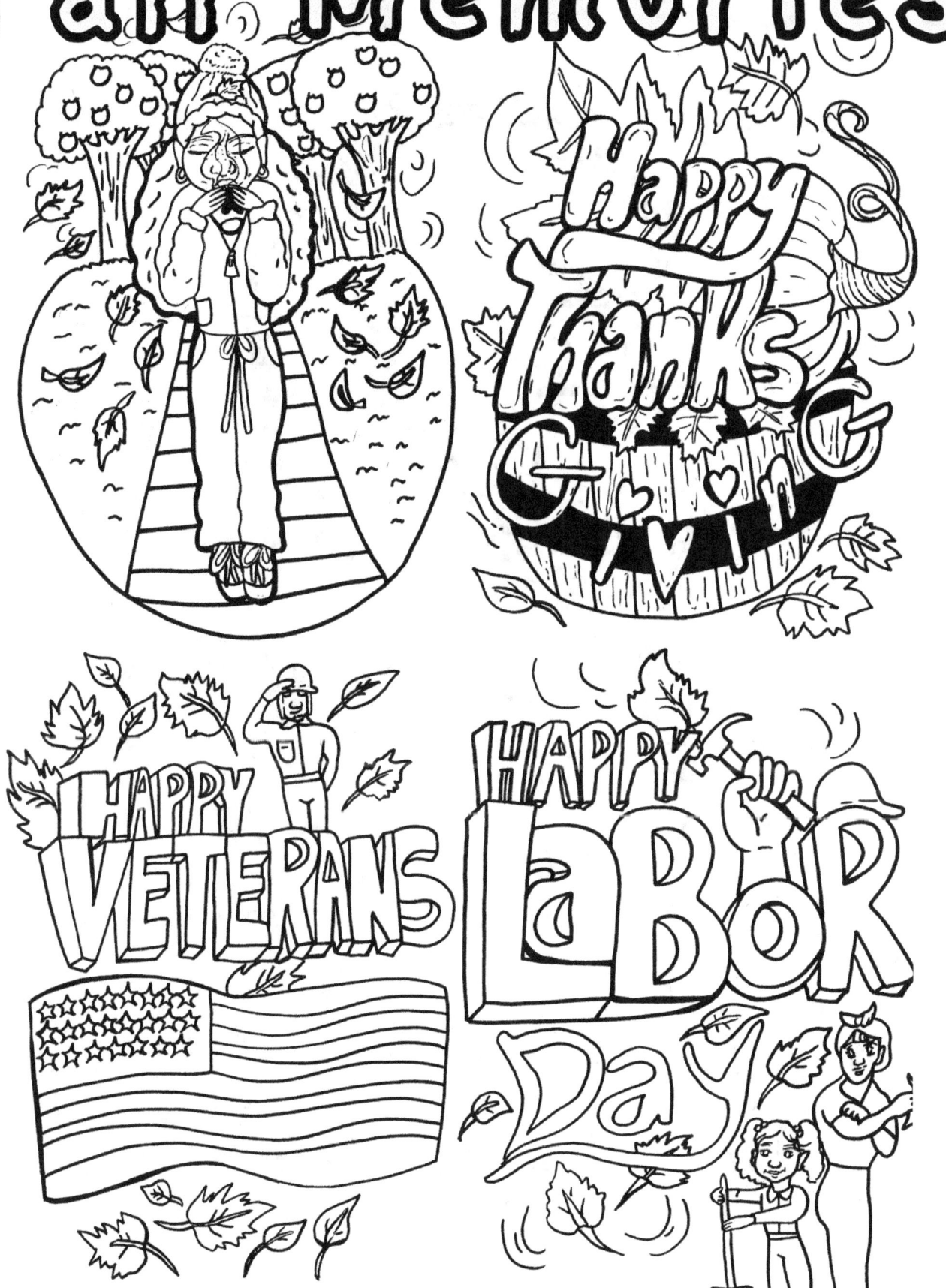

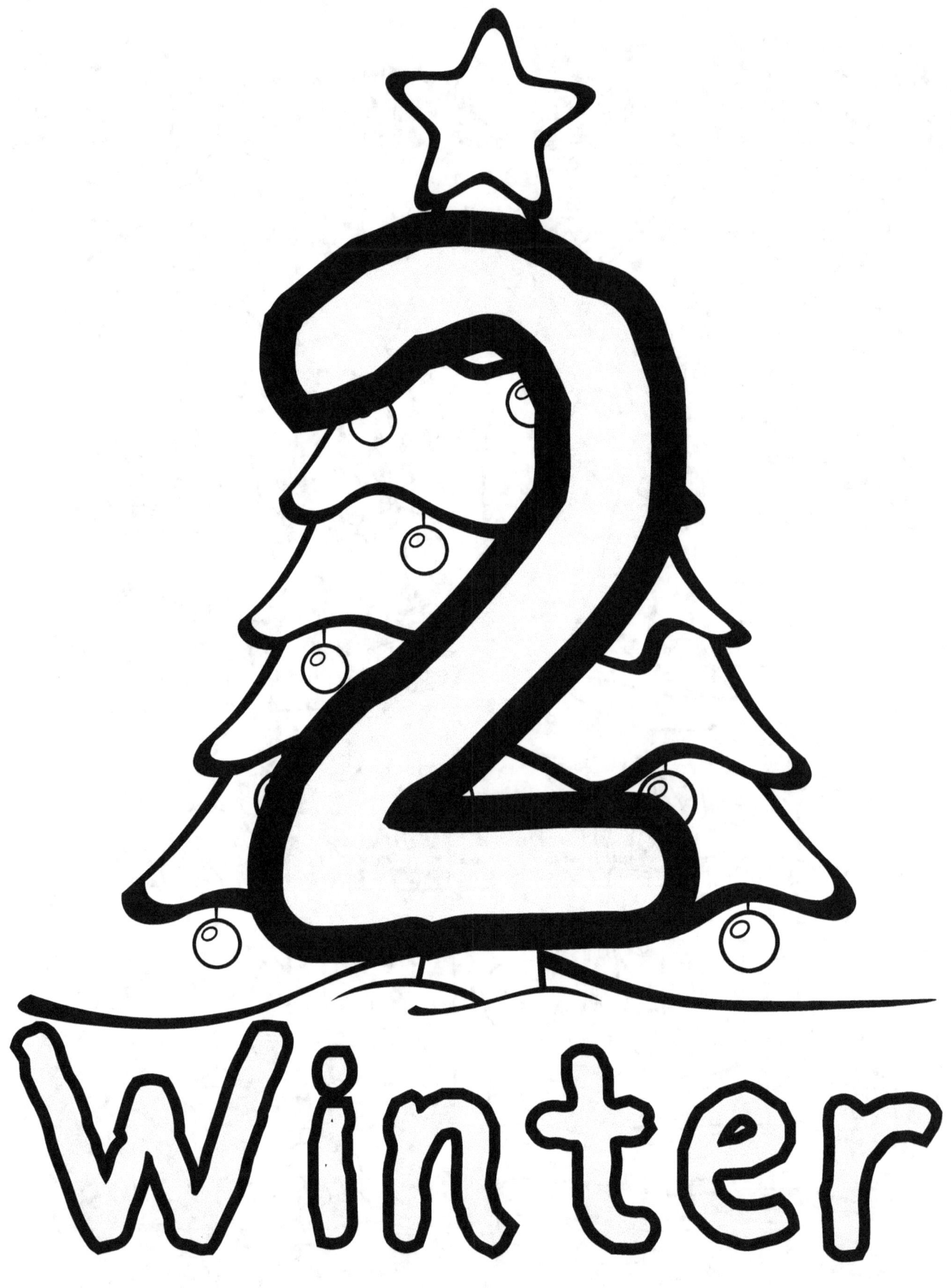

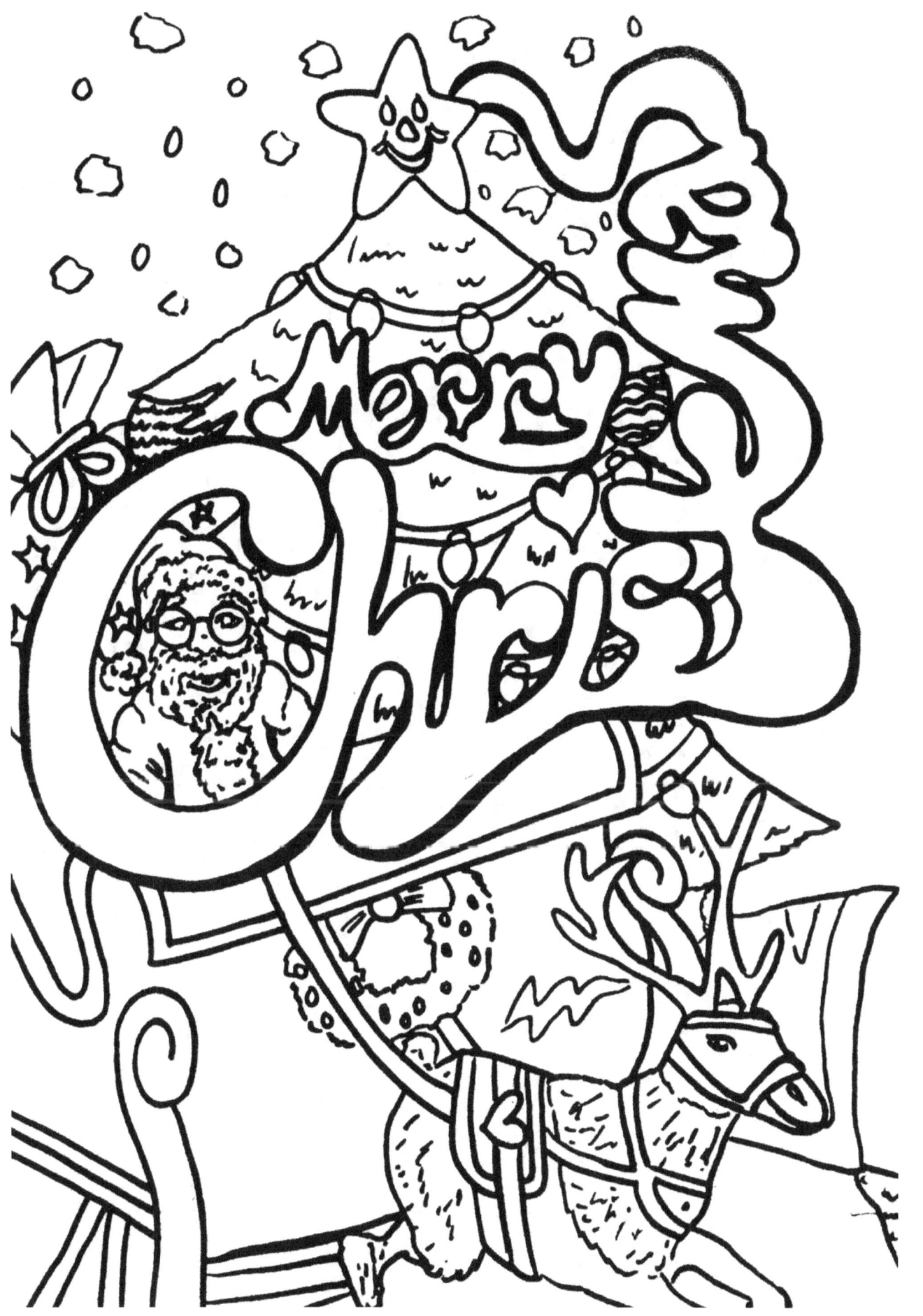

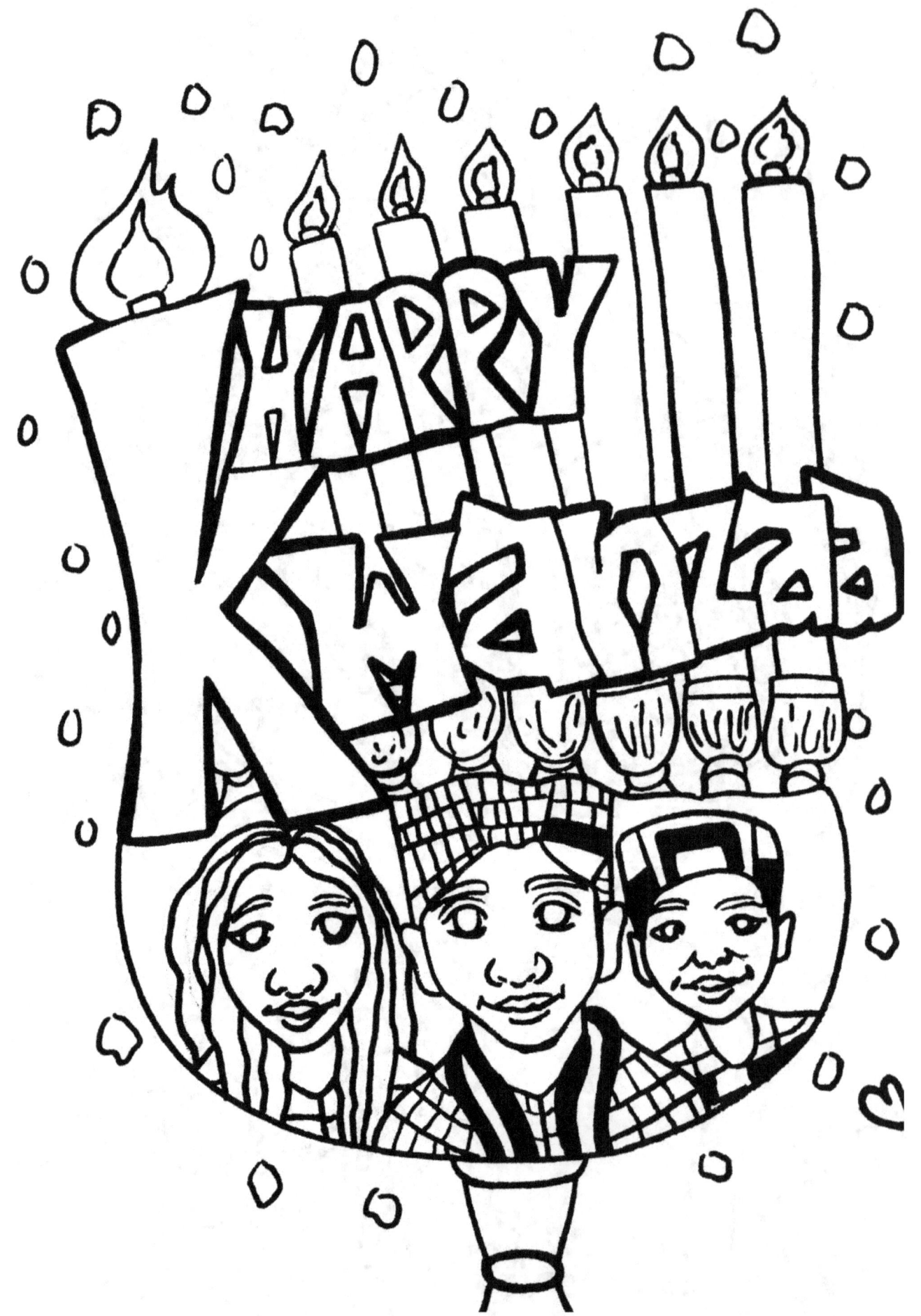

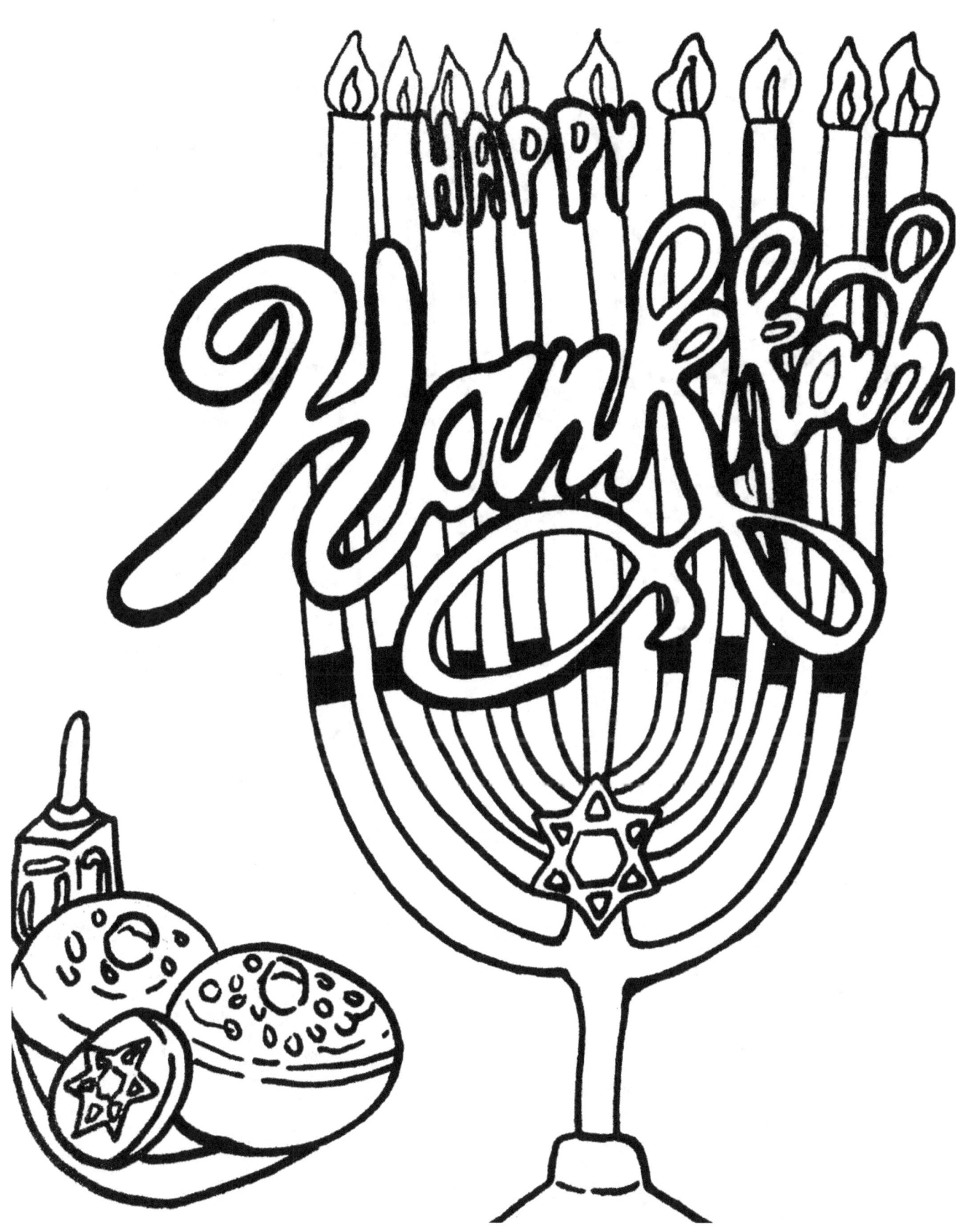

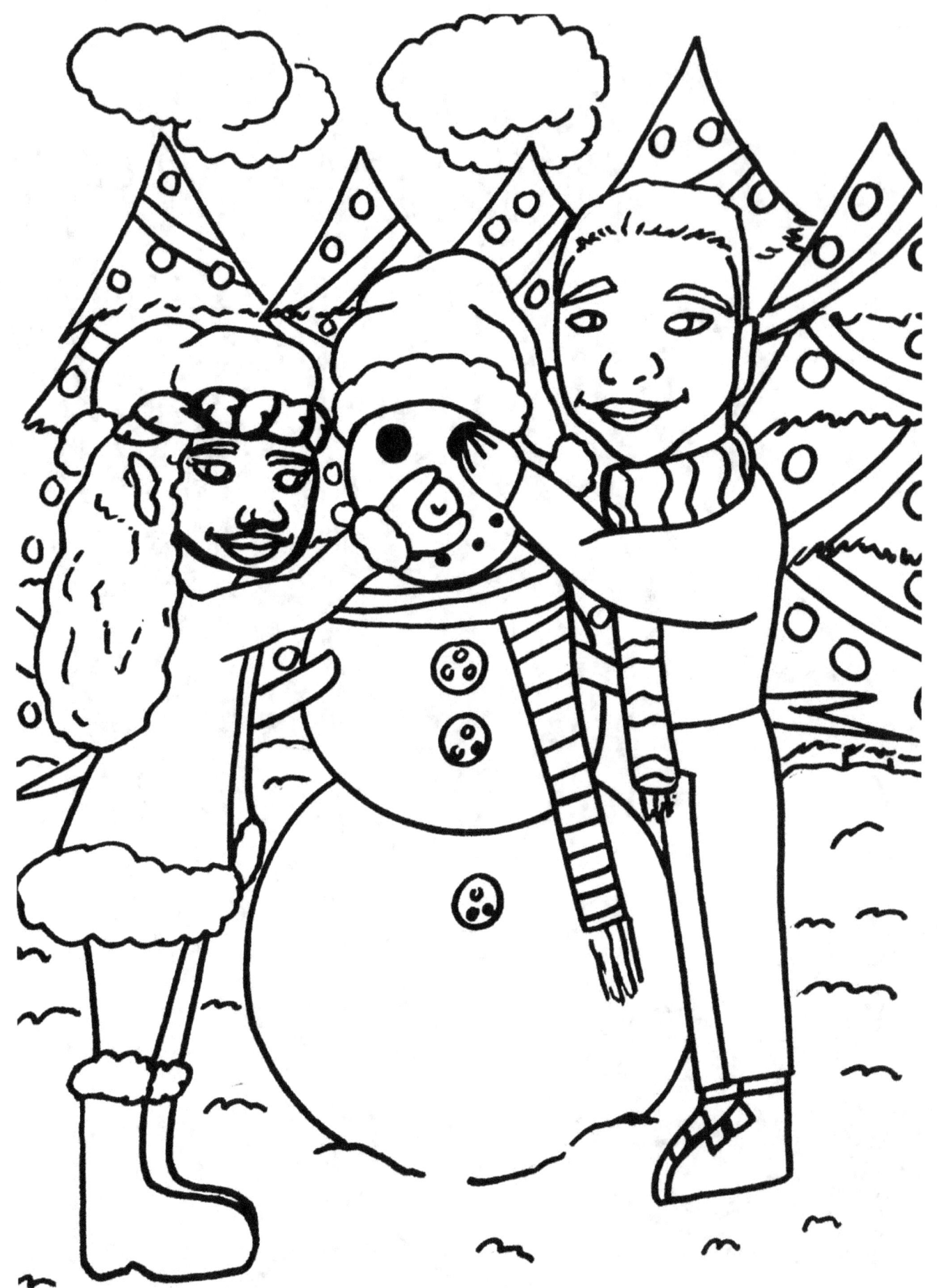

Winter Memories

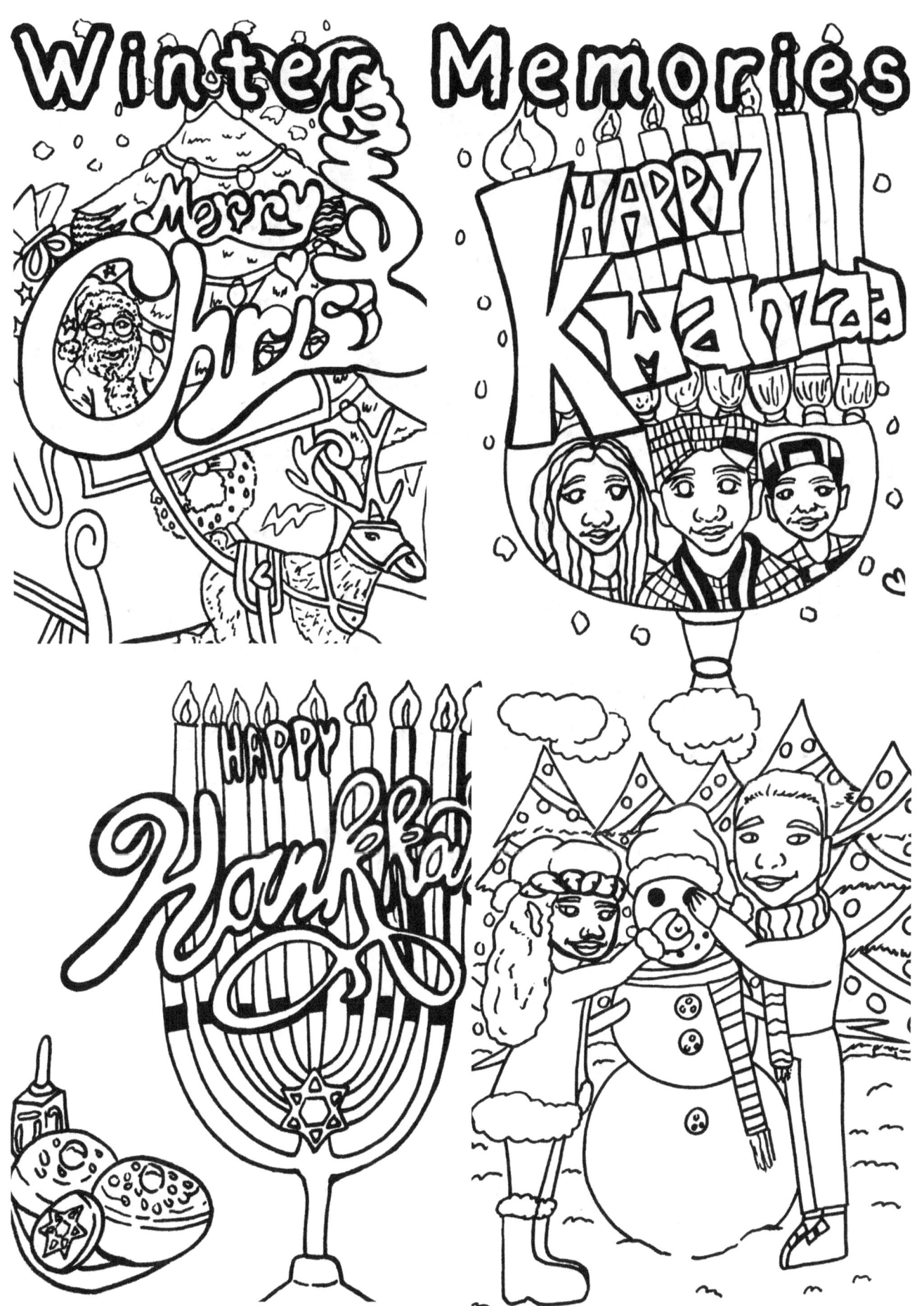

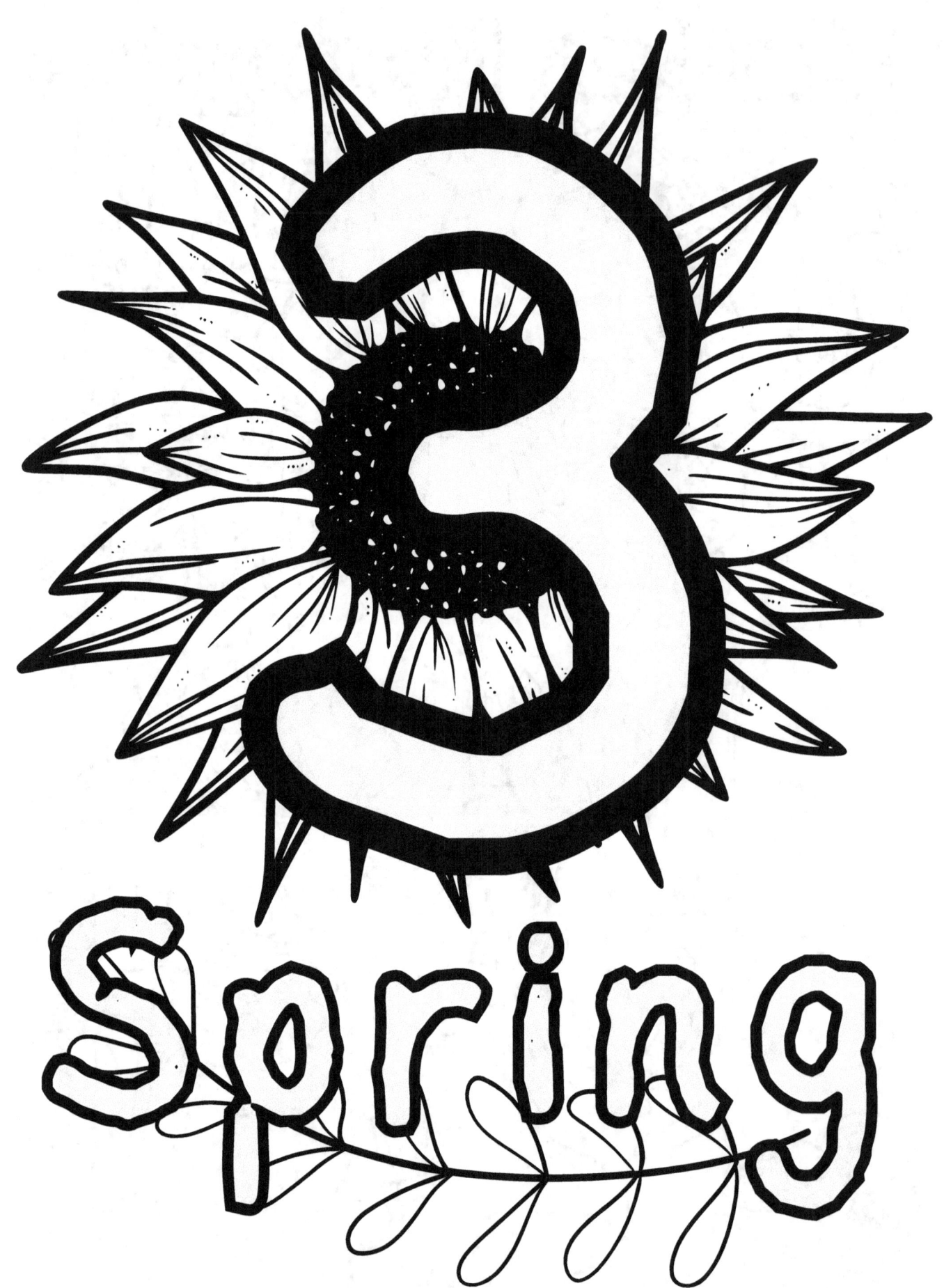

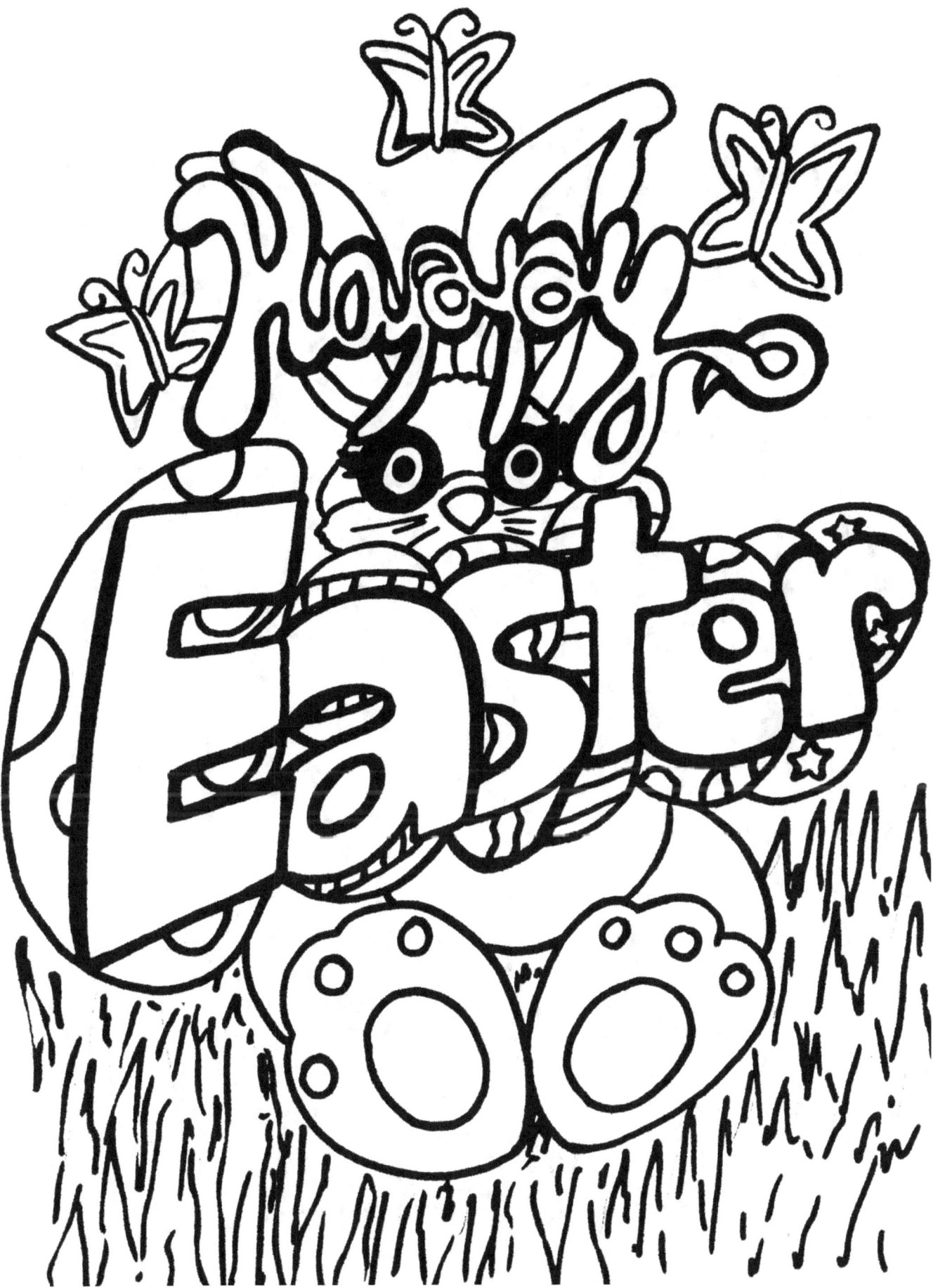

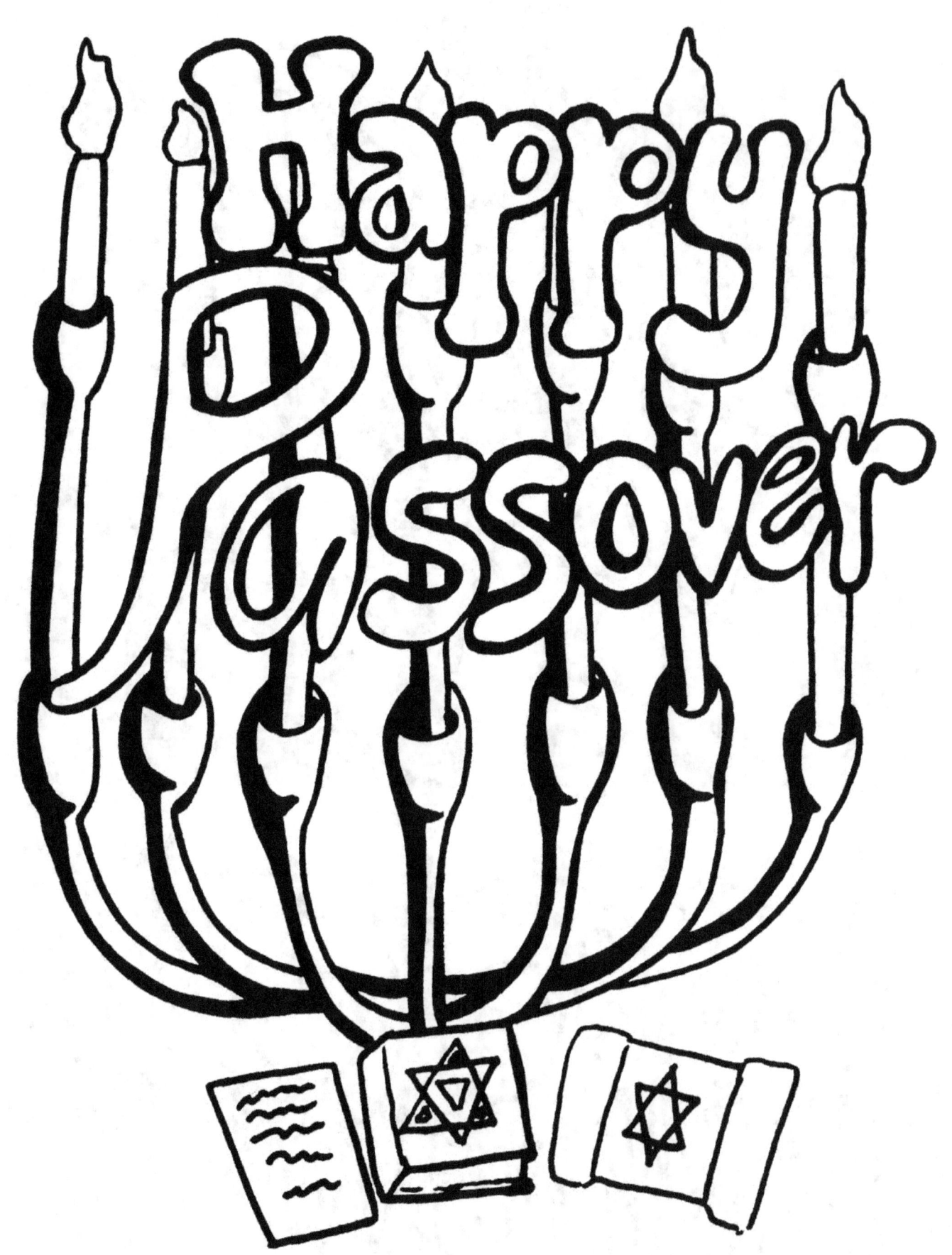

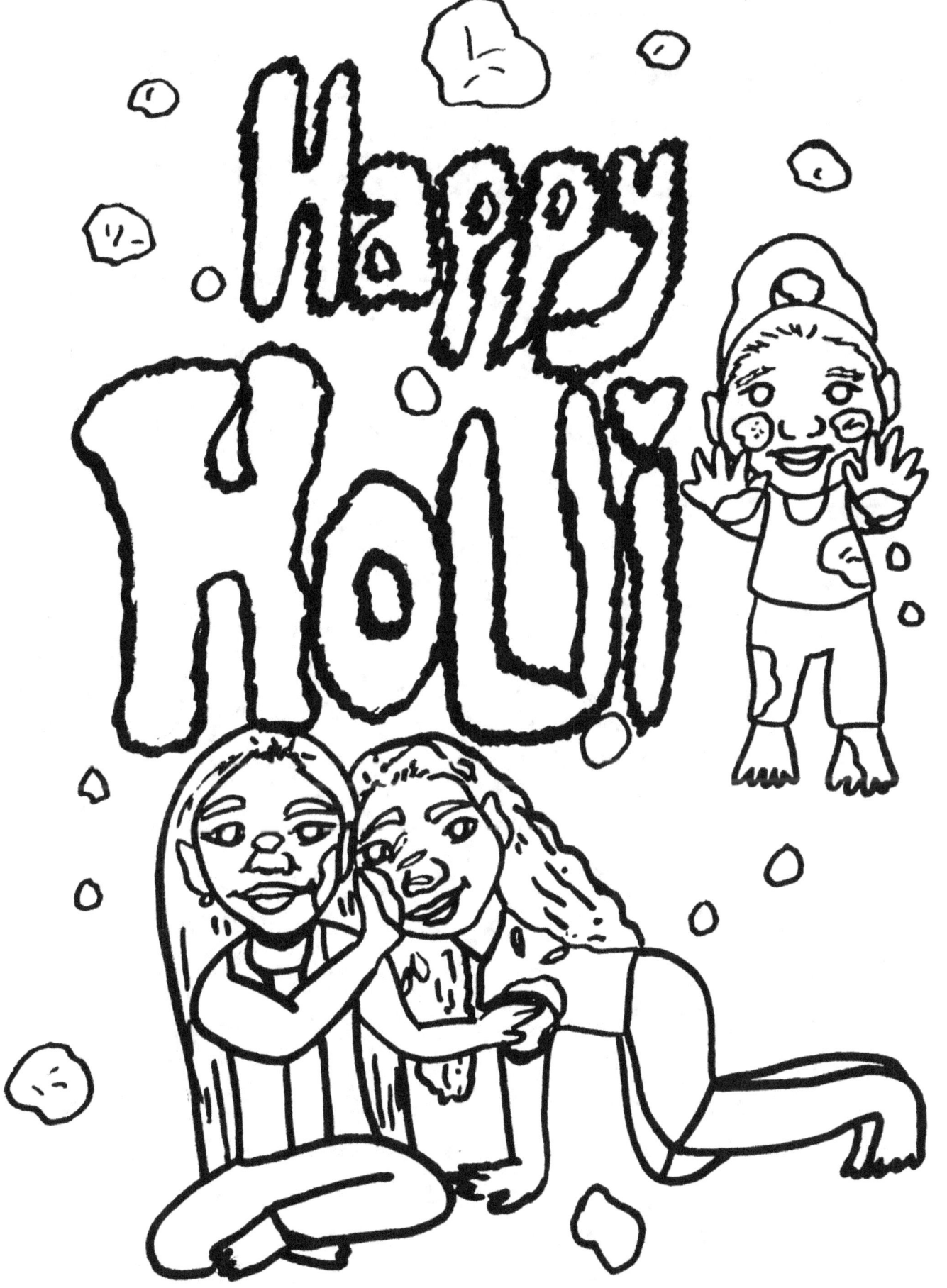

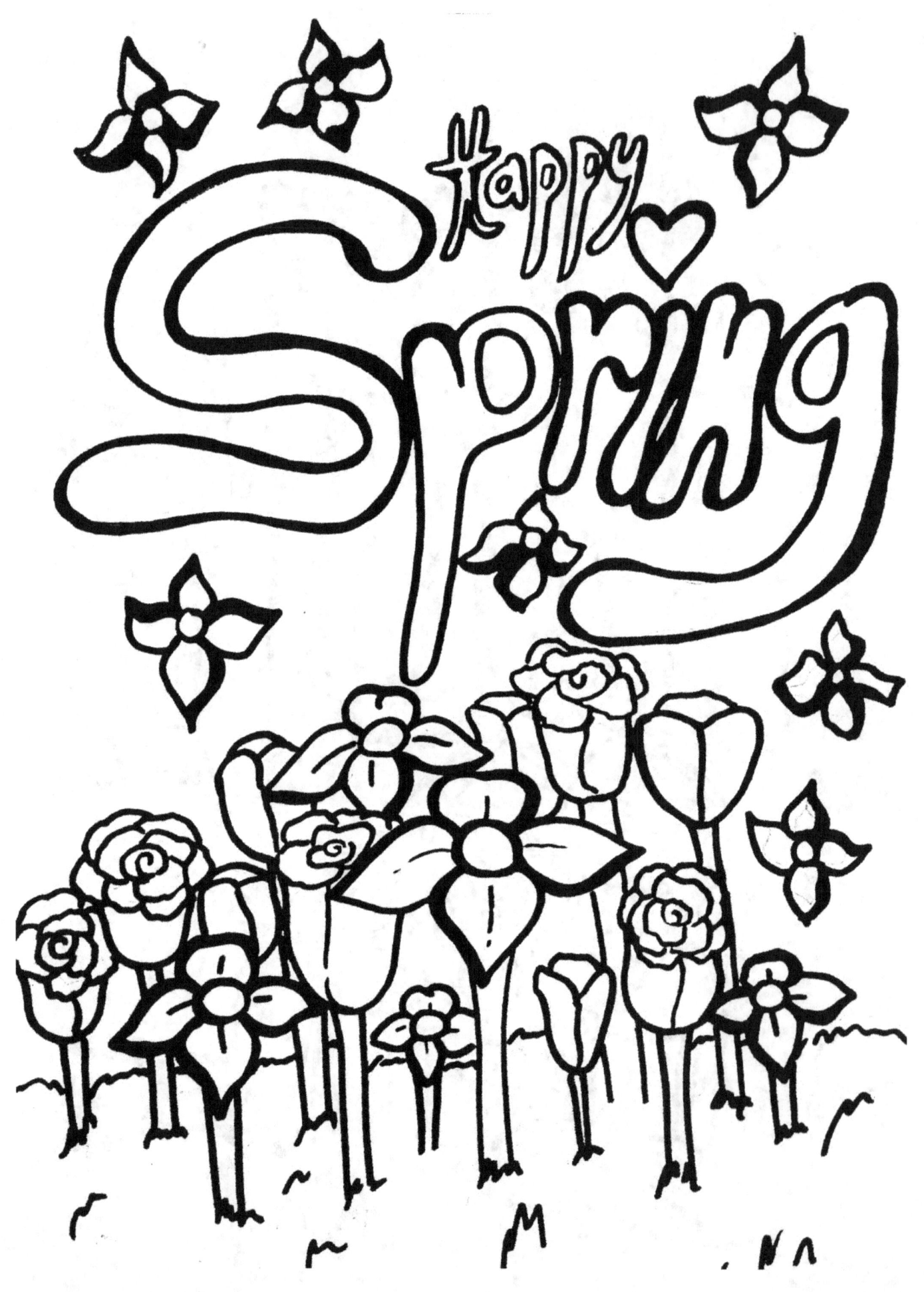

Spring Memories

Happy **Easter**

Happy Passover

Happy **Holi**

Happy **Spring**

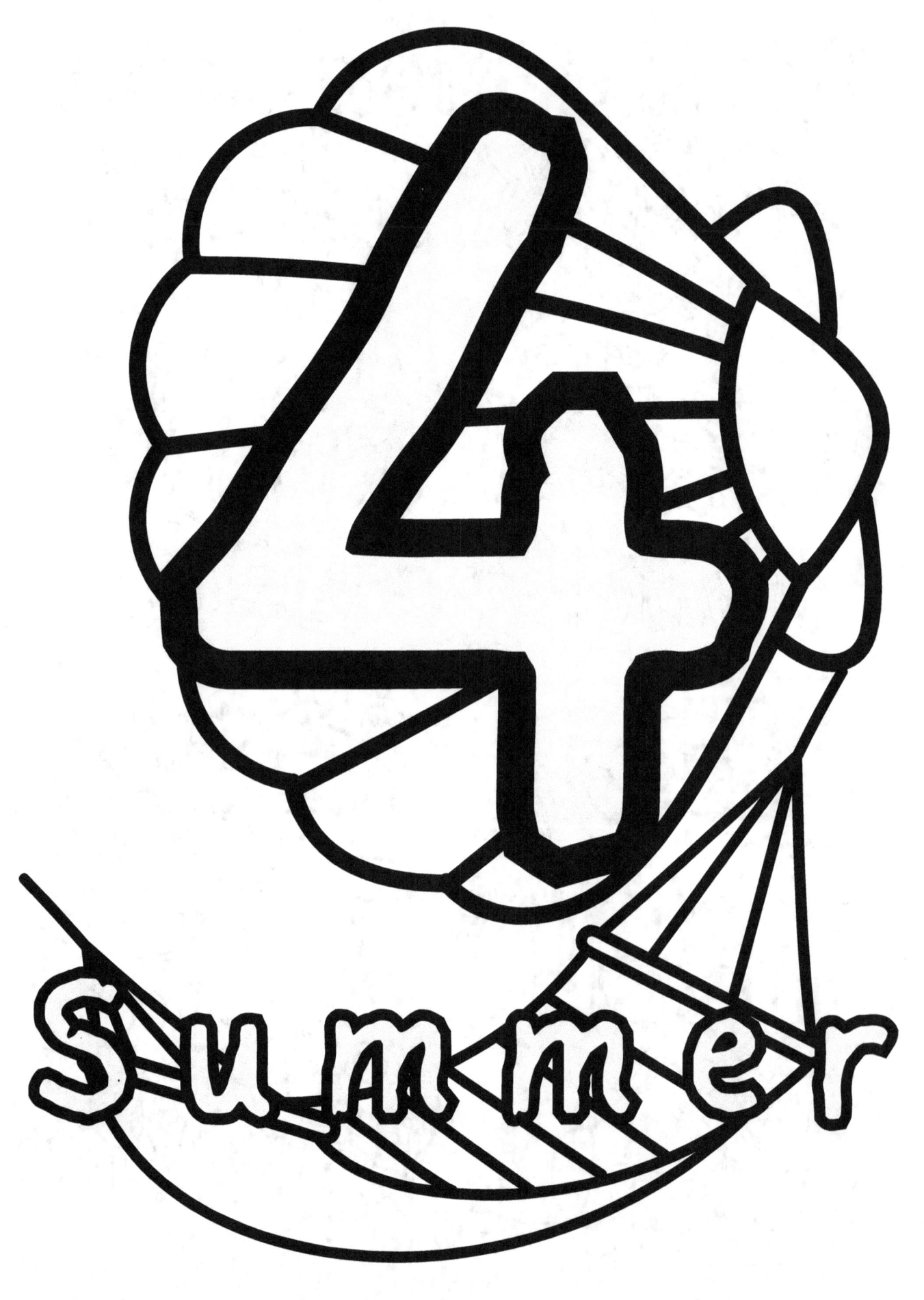

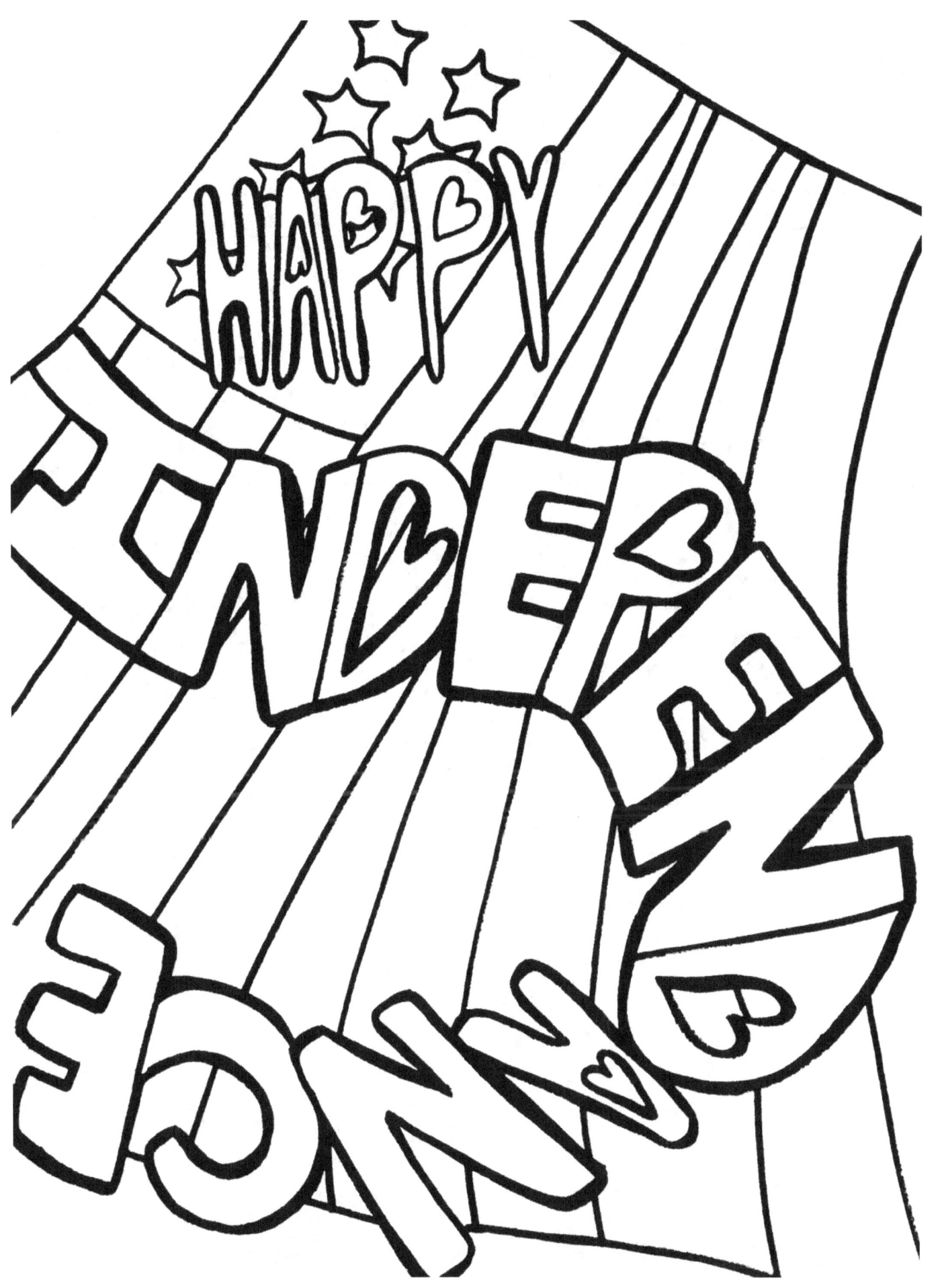

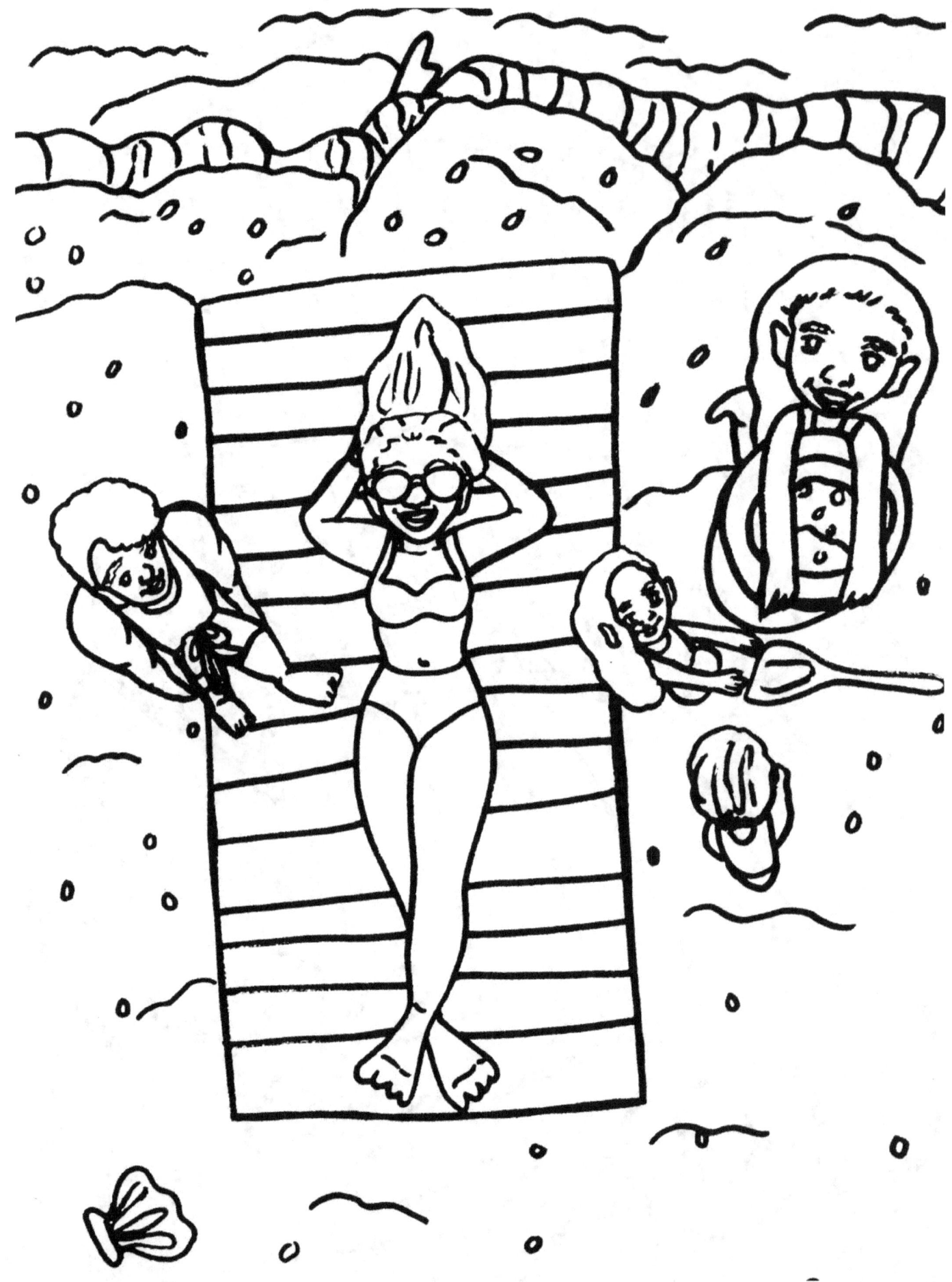

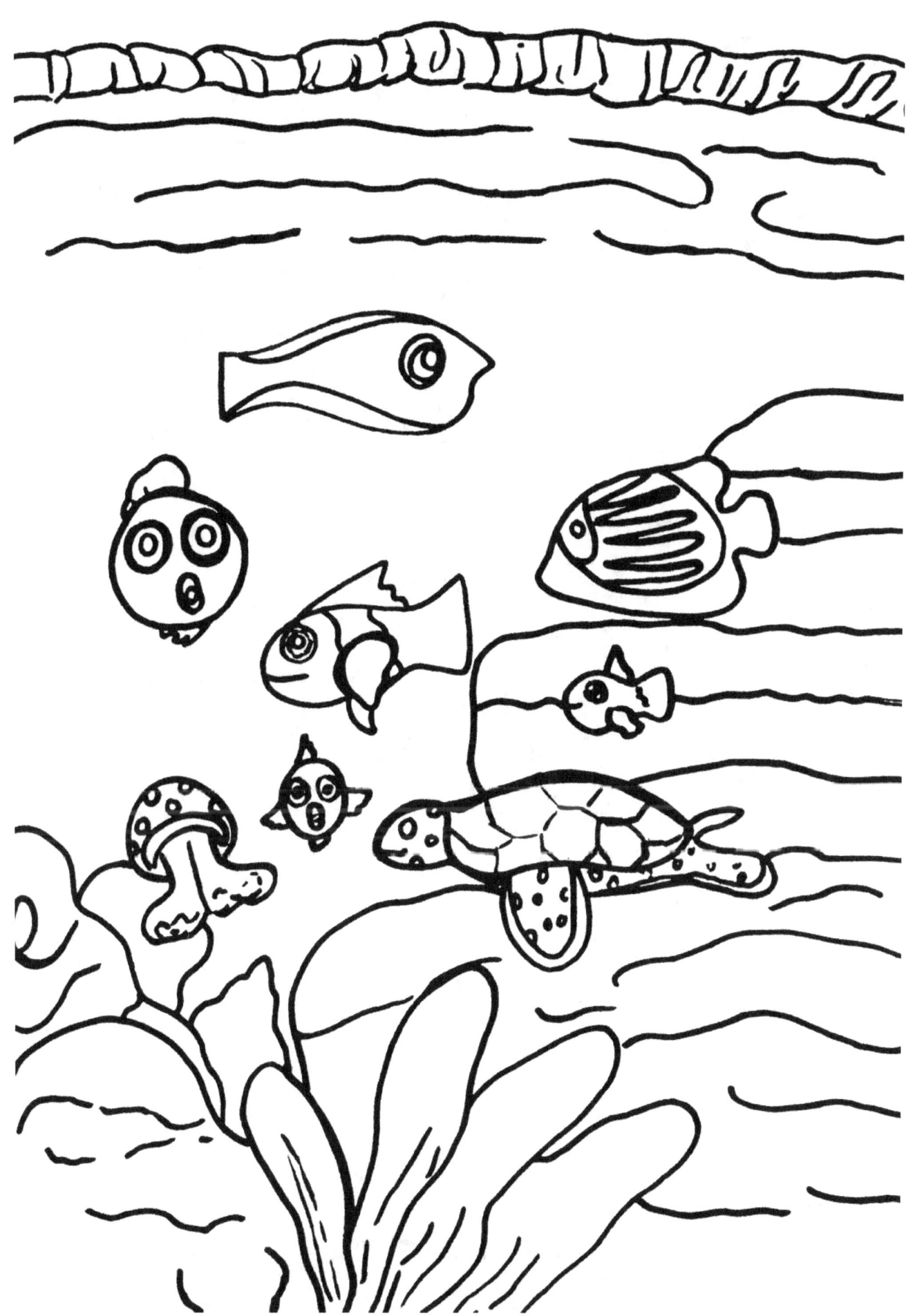

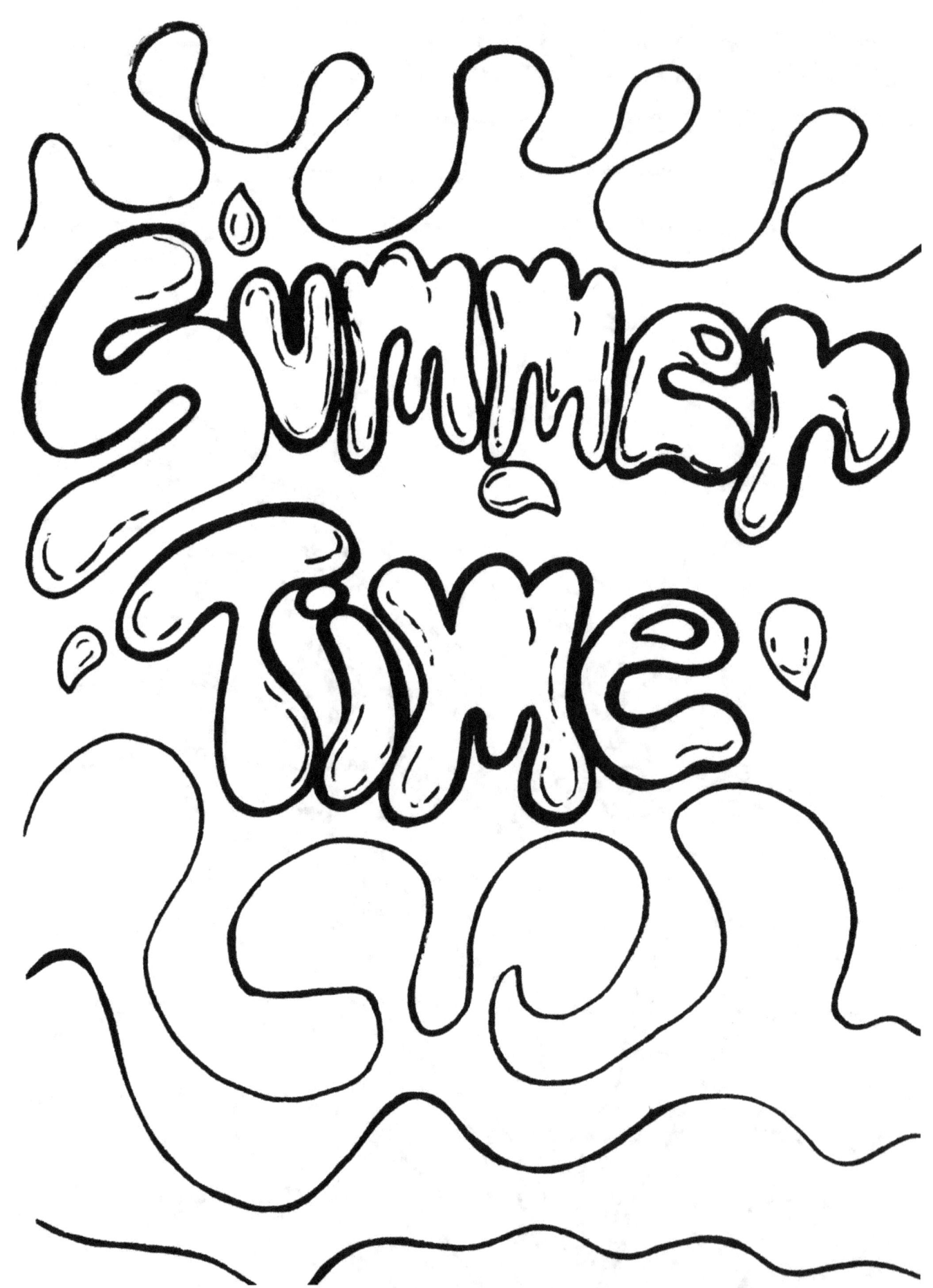

Summer Memories

HAPPY INDEPENDENCE

Summer Time